"One day you will make peace with your demons, and the chaos in your heart will settle flat. Then, the world will smile back, and welcome you home"

- R.M. Drake

ISLE OF SKYE

— NATALIE NASCENZI —

PUBLISHING

ii Publishing
New York, NY

www.toniiinc.com

Cover art by Nicolle Dilorio

Cover design by tonii

ISBN: 978-1-7362167-9-8

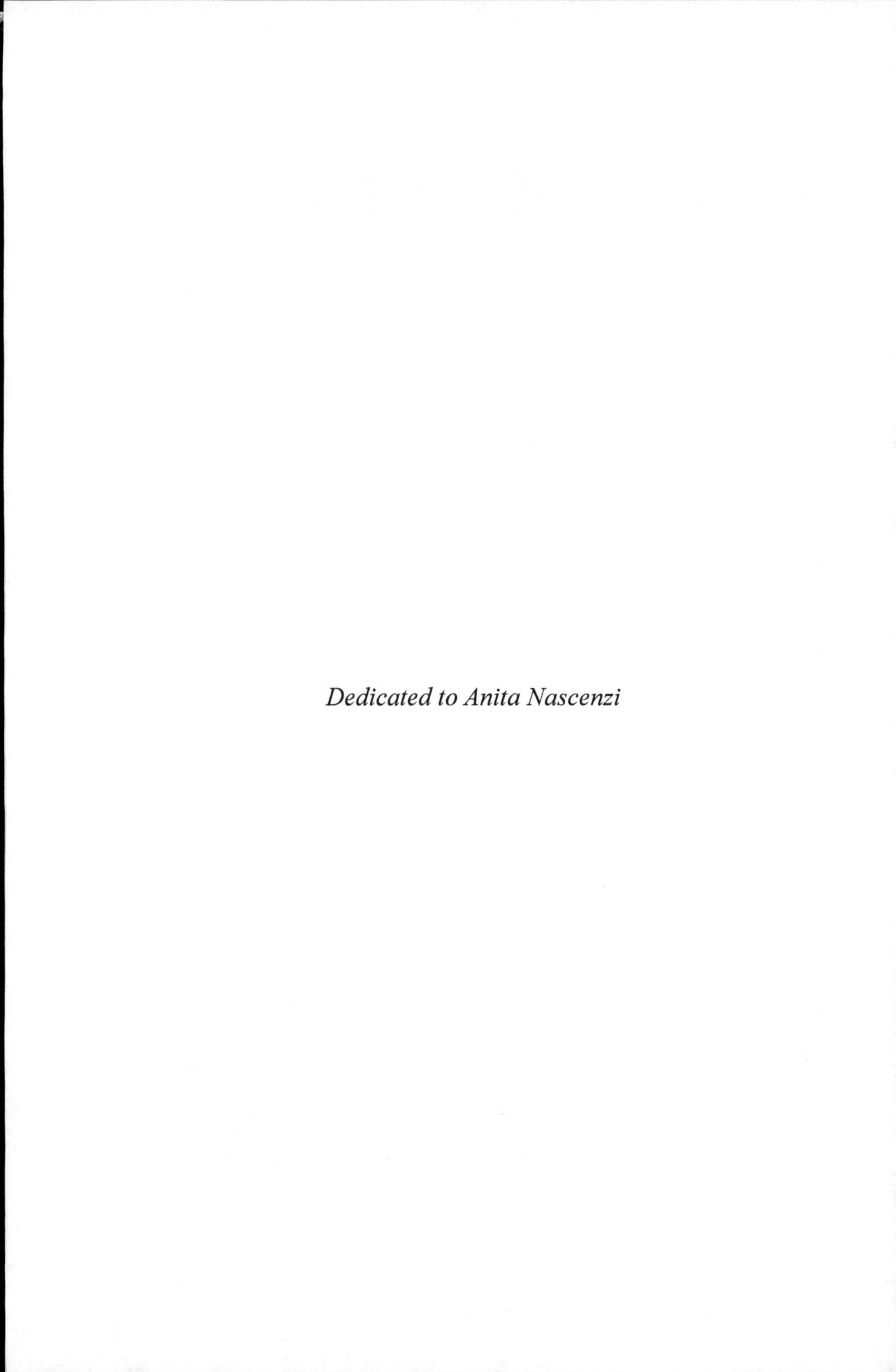

Dedicated to Anita Nascenzi

TITLE THE CONTENTS

As you read through these pages, I invite you to name the poems as you go, based on your connection with the words.

1. ____
2. ____
3. ____
4. ____
5. ____
6. ____
7. ____
8. ____
9. ____
10. ____
11. ____
12. ____
13. ____
14. ____
15. ____
16. ____
17. ____

18. ____

19. ____

20. ____

21. ____

22. ____

23. ____

24. ____

25. ____

26. ____

27. ____

28. ____

29. ____

30. ____

31. ____

32. ____

33. ____

34. ____

35. ____

36. ____

37. ____

38. ____

39. ____

40. ____

41. ____

42. ____

43. ____

44. ____

45. ____

46. ____

47. ____

48. ____

49. ____

50. ____

51. ____

52. ____

53. ____

54. ____

55. ____

56. ____

57. ____

58. ____

59. ____

60. ____

61. ____

62. ____

63. ____

64. ____

65. ____

66. ____

67. ____

68. ____

69. ____

SHARE YOUR TABLE OF CONTENTS & TAG ME.

@nncenzi

@natalie.nascenzi

@ncenzi

...the beginning...

Leap of Faith

I stood at the edge of "what's next..."

...and I pondered
Looking down at the uncharted waters
Standing in place is secure and safe
Yet, I wonder… what lies at the bottom?

At the edge of this cliff is unsettling
There below me, a sea of unknown
If I jump I'll end up swimming *somewhere*
To a place I can finally call home

The thrilling idea of this freedom
A vision, a life that's brand new
It's a risky decision, letting go of the past
But it seems like the right thing to do

With wonder and courage, I whisper,
"You'll never know unless you try."
Then, I take a deep breath
Off the edge, I step

And instead of falling…I fly...

To the Isle of Skye...

Dear Reader,

Today is August 1, 2021.

I began my poetic journey exactly three years ago to this day. I sat at the park down the street from my apartment and decided that I was going to make my first book, OUT OF CHAOS a reality. *I decided to take a leap of faith.* Looking back on that moment, I never could have imagined the ripple effect of that one simple decision. The single idea of writing a poetry book changed my entire life. *This is a very important message my friends:* **The decisions you make, right now, will sow the seeds for your future; whatever you decide to do today has the power to redirect your entire course.**

The story that has unfolded over the past three years has been nothing short of a miracle. If you've been following my journey—from weight loss to depression, stage fright to spotlight, through the pandemic and into The Aftermath of Unrest, you'll very well know the incredible circumstances that have guided me along my path. God has a funny way of working through people, experiences, and opportunities—all of which have been captured in both of my previous books.

However, if you're coming from Out of Chaos or the Aftermath of Unrest, expecting to read about what happened next, I would like you to know…that is simply not the case with this book.

Once The Aftermath of Unrest was published, my plan was to immediately capture what happened next in a third and final book. Unfortunately, the words never came. As time passed, it became very clear that I couldn't write about what was happening because that part of my poetic journey had already ended.

An entirely new adventure had begun, one that I will need to live *first* and write *later*. This time, I'd like to let it simply happen.

This book contains both the said and the unsaid. It is a collection of everything I have written that has not been published or earned its place in one of my books. It is comprised of pain, joy, and healing. It is *everything* I have left to share before I can step into an entirely new world of poetry and possibility.

Every beginning starts with a leap of faith and the absolute trust that even though the journey will take you through the chaotic unknown— eventually everything falls into place.

One way or another, we all get to where we're going.

Even though it's bittersweet to step away from what we know and say goodbye to an old version of ourselves, it is important to remember:

The end is only just the beginning.

Love always,

1

Blinded by the doubt within
That clouds what you perceive
If you see through my eyes
You'll have vision—clear and free

Twisted words and wicked tongue
Stained by evil thoughts
If you speak through my lips
You'll never once feel lost

Deafened by surrounding cries
Of voices, not your own
But if you listen with my ears

You'll never feel alone.

Meri aankhon se dekho.

2

"Today I saw you dancing
Entangled in the rain
Spinning under storm clouds
With a smile on your face
Can you explain?"

"Yes...

It's called waltzing with the rainfall
Each step is quite intense
You match the liquid beat beneath your feet
As the droplets kiss cement."

3

Beside me, a flock of reflections
All variations of me
The shells of my past
Build a shield

Now, impossible to defeat.

4

I may have jumped the gun
Went soaring to conclusions
I was caught in wicked ways
And all my minds confusions

My back was turned
My eyes were closed
I somehow missed the message
Oh shit, it's just, I didn't think...
Oh shit, I might regret this...

Maybe I should just admit

You've always left me breathless

......

Oh shit, I may have got it wrong
Resurrected my defenses
Unprepared, soul screamed

"Beware! Love comes with consequences."

Now it's much too late to act
Take back my second guessing
Nothing less, I must accept
That love is just a lesson

So, I'll sip my midnight coffee, and then

I'll count each blessing.

✴

5

Your world
My world
The worlds in between
Separately orbit alone
Then, there's a place
That's just yours and mine
And that— is a world of its own

Mix worlds
My life
Your people
Sprinkled in little by little

Your life
My people
So different...

Yet somehow, we meet in the middle
Sometimes the fates don't blend quite right
Two lives don't seem to match
We face the choice to let it be
Or decide it's the time to retract

Own world
One person
Lone spirit
Bouncing between all the places

There's plenty that seem
Like the right place to be
Just be careful with whom you trade faces

It's important to note this one simple fact
Always keep this truth in mind:

There are simply some worlds and people...

That are never meant to collide.

6

I feel too much and think too hard
My brain is an endless maze
I try to feel nothing, it ends up pointless
And so, I get caught in a craze
My head and its reckless ways

I restlessly wander around
I've found that I fall too quickly
Then get mad when my face hits the ground

I trip over my feelings
Get lost in the moment
Run away when I can't get it straight
This chaos inside, seems to never subside
When it does
I am always too late

"Just say it!"
I scream from the inside
Trying to break down my walls
I have to be clear, face what I fear
And just say it
Once and for all…

But, I trip and I fall
Staring up at the words from below
I open my mouth
And all that comes out

Is a stupid, awkward "Hello."

7

I sip magic
Laced with insane
Chase with the truth

And let it seep through my veins.

8

Twirling over city streets
Swirling in the breeze
Whisking by, unbothered
Prancing with the leaves

Flowing with the winds
Drifting by, unfettered
My effortless dance with the singing winds
I, the floating feather

Where I go, always unknown
Unsure of where I'll land
And just as I'm about to fall

There is always a change in the wind.

9

"Who made a beautiful woman like you cry?"

I sigh, wipe the streaks that stain my face
"Well, I thought I got it right this time...
But... that's simply not the case."

I relied too much on fate, tried to speak the truth
Was greeted by: "You're just too nice,
Too kind, too absolute."

"Too nice is not a bad thing. What makes you so upset?"
"Well, I've re-lived the moment many times
So, they're tears of pure *regret*."

"Regret?" "Yes."

"I said I'd never feel again, it'd be me, myself, and I...
Foolishly, I broke my rule—the first reason why I cried."

"Hmmm someone as 'too nice' as you...doesn't need that guy."

"*Oh*...I know," I crack a smile,
"*That's the other reason why.*"

10

An electric shock to the iris
Your cosmic eyes meet mine
A million passing faces

And it's just you and I.

11

I know it may sound silly
But, there's no way to deny this
It seems like wishful thinking
But actually—*it's science*

This simple scientific fact
Is one we can't avoid:

The energy around us is not created or destroyed

Science or insanity
You choose which to believe
But, to break the laws of physics
Seems atrociously obscene

You see, the energy between us
Somewhere still exists
It might not be so tangible
Until you reminisce...

And so, I state my premise:
Forever in this reverie,
Our energy was not destroyed

It only became my memory

12

That girl will write you
She'll brand you as a poem
Slay you with a felt-tip pen
The words she's left unspoken

She'll immortalize your memory
Scribble out your faults
Rewrite you as the sunset
See the good and nothing else

She'll turn her pain to poetry
The pen will sing your praise
You'll wonder why she flipped the script
And beautified your ways

The ink that stings her fingertips
Turns perspicacious prose
A river—pain to power
And from her pen it flows

Her scars are scraps of paper
Her words waltz off the page
And, when the curtain draws
She'll be standing on the stage

Proudly pronouncing every line
That's dripping with your name
The part you'll never understand?
Her words are not in vain

She pens them as a lesson
Proclaims them, unashamed
For her words are not a weapon
They reflect her wisdom gained.

13

Standing at the ocean's edge
Surrounded by salty breeze
I told you I'd be waiting
Where the sunset kissed the seas

I told you that I'd be here
Between the shades of blue
Where horizon meets the tie-dyed clouds
As the sunset blends its hues

The most breath taking of views
And I'm waiting there for you
Aren't you coming?

I'm confused

It won't be that much longer
The crashing waves sing louder
Washing away the sands of time
As I wait through the golden hour

The sun is swallowed by the tides
The moon begins to rise
A waterfall of scattered stars
Begins to fill the skies

Silently, I cried

Forever I have waited
For you to be here by my side
it might be time to finally admit

That you might not arrive.

14

"Try writing about love.."

"Okay…"

I see a smile in your iris
As it reflects the golden skies
They catch the sun and sing a tune
The song of a sparkling eyes

My concrete heart cracks open
By your electrifying essence
The walls I've built fall crumbling down
And shatter in your presence

…

….

I'm sorry…but that's all I've got
Cause' when push comes to shove
I'd rather write my madness

Than pretend that I'm in love.

15

Bounding down a straight narrow path
and I came to a startling halt.

Before me a towering mountain
and on each side, the path splits off.

I stood there for quite some time
unsure of the road which to travel.

Overthinking the right path to pick
as I kicked at the grass and the gravel.

"Which way?" I pondered, obsessively
I weighed what I'd win and lose...

Concluded that climbing up, over the mountain
meant that I won't have to choose.

But, it also meant an unpaved path
with dangerous, rugged terrain.

The unknown outcome of freedom...
a choice-less, exciting escape.

So, I ran to the base and began to climb
to the top in a restless pursuit.

It's an obstacle course and a much tougher route…

An adventure I couldn't refuse.

16

I waited for you in the moonlight

I waited.....

But you never came

Hopeful, I searched for your shadow
A pawn, in your maddening game

Under a dazzling blanket of stars
My fingers entwined in the grass
Keeping my hopeful hands occupied
Open wide with nothing to grasp

The seasons are changing
I'm waiting
Years, in the blink of an eye
I waited
And waited
How foolish
To let my whole life pass me by–

Waiting patiently for nothing to arrive.

17

I'm often inspired by the crystal abyss
A brilliant moon in an ocean of stars
Sometimes I ponder electrons
Or, how protons stay positively charged

Sometimes it hits
While I randomly sit
Looking into a galaxy of steel
Peering at checkerboard lights from a tower
Thinking…

"How in the world do I feel?"

It could be bird
Or a sandwich
A pile of trash on the street
Most of the time I'm inspired
By a stranger I randomly meet

But lately, I'm crazy and all bottled up
The engine inside has misfired
Quite possibly so, I may need a nap

I'm much too tired to be re-inspired.

18

"What are you writing?"

I don't know

"Is it love?"

I only write pain

"Is it love that you're writing?"

It's nothing.

I look back at the page, and it's blank.

"Why are you here?"

I don't know

"Why are you here and not home?"

Well, I sit and write nothing in silence

Because it's better than being alone

"What do you want?"

I don't know...

"State your business"

I haven't a clue

"What were you writing?"

Madness, that is, until I came here and met you

See…all I have written is loneliness
And, I came here to sit—*just because*
My business is no expectations
Then, I ended up writing down "love"

I stared at the word
Fiddled my pen
Chatted with people that passed
Sipped on my coffee, felt nothing

I only tried to write "love" cause *you* asked.

19

No longer afraid of the fire before me
The unwritten song that life sings
I have walked through flames
Scarred—yet unscathed

I learned how to rule from within

The curb, the concrete, the city street

Like my heart

Cracked yet, strong

A steady beat once tuned by defeat..

Now plays me a beautiful song.

20

Red means go
Green means stop
See... *love* sounds like *evil*
To all broken hearts

Yellow is stagnant
Caught up in the middle
Confusion and chaos

From disordered signals.

21

Forbidden body
Lonely touch
Smiling shadow
Crimson flush

Silent darkness
Silver moon
Sparkling ocean
Smoky room

Quiet madness
Tender bliss
Soft and steady
Breathless kiss

Heartless harmony
Dancing limbs
Electric movements
Skin to skin

Wild iris
Daring grin
Call it love

Or is it sin?

22

Racing thoughts
Restless night
The clock strikes 1am
They say that time can heal the mind
Yet, I can't sleep...*again*

Sirens shake the city awake
Chaos breaks the silence
When it comes to thoughts and feelings

They're the only thing that's timeless.

23

I once stood across the street...

In front of an old moment
That was somehow lost in time
I catch a glimpse of yesterday
And then, the clock rewinds

There I stand
Unknowingly
No clue of what's to come
But now, here in the present
The bigger picture comes undone

A vision of my past self
If only she could see
That although the moment holds her
She's where she needs to be

This note from future you:
The road ahead is full of fear
But if you choose to face the fire
Then I'll be waiting here.

24

Drop your shield and flaming blade
Dismount, assume the position
You must learn to slay the ego

Using only intuition.

25

Drop the veil
Shed your cloak
Stand up
Collect your rose
Valiantly face the sun
To leave your waiting post

Look back and blow a kiss
To lessons of endless searching
Your unclipped wings
Now free to soar
A bird, no longer perching

A lifetime of observing
From high above the ground
Embracing sky and taking flight

What was lost, has now been found.

26

Here is the fact of the matter
I come with no terms or conditions
There are simply no rules, I float with the wind
I live freely without supervision

Please understand my insanity
Get to know my restless soul
I promise, I always return
It's just my nature to come and then go

I rise with the sun every morning
I'm up and I'm out before dawn
Filling my eyes with the lavender skies
Then I'm back, before you notice I'm gone

You'll find me with coffee and waffles
Reading and writing till noon
I never quite know where the day's gonna go
It's an "up-in-the-air" rendezvous

I don't follow rules, I don't status quo
And I live outside of the "box"
To me, every day's an adventure
They all end with the sun as it sets

One more fact, there is a catch
No rules, except one, or I flee:
I'll be the best thing that happens to you...

Don't be the worst thing that happens to me.

27

Bippity Boppity Boo

I'm harnessing the darkness
I cannot be it
Or misuse it
See, there are demons in my mind

But in my headphones...
Disney music.

28

You see,
Meteors are fleeting

They flash
Then crash to earth
So fast we seem to miss the fact
Of the moment and its worth

We reminisce its brilliance
Wonder why we can't forget it
Well, after making an impact
It's a meteorite…

Now, magnetic.

29

"I waited for thousands of years…

I prayed for the stars to align

Watched you across the galaxy

Hoping someday we'd collide

The galaxy swirling us closer

Gravity, intense and divine

Mesmerized, waiting for thousands of years

And now the day has finally arrived."

-Jupiter to Saturn

30

Autopilot mindset
Soul on cruise control
You fall in line with moving crowds
Complacent and composed

Tunnel visionary
Doomed to be confined
Frantically glancing down at glass
As hands tick by the time

The world moves on around you
Glazes by in motion
Painted with a steady blur
A living, breathing, ocean

Of all the same people.

31

I asked the world for a message
As I sat, with my mind torn apart
Then, I unwrapped a dove chocolate
And the wrapper said,

"Follow your heart"

It's hard to hear my heartbeat
When mind gets in the way
Erratic beating
Mixed with metal repeating
At a loss from the words I should say

My mind is chaotic
Firing lies
My thoughts reject and betray
But the sweetness of clarity
Sings me a story:

That the heart cannot lead you astray.

32

Smoldering battlegrounds
Billowing smoke
Fire
Sirens blaring
Cackling wood and embers

The aftershock of fury

Wading through the aftermath
Tightly grasping passion
From this field of fire

And rising from the ashes.

33

The shadow of your cheekbones
Amidst the moonless sky
The constellations shape your face
The stars, your contoured lines

Galactic eyes stare into mine
Entranced, I trace your face
Lost inside the orbit
Of star-crossed, twisted fate

Outlined in the exosphere
The diamond studded abyss
Your stellar silhouette
Has left my soul eclipsed.

34

I will not acquiesce
Or submit to "status quo"
If that does not sit well with you
Then, I'll just stand alone

A dog without a collar
A muzzle
Or a leash
I will not be guided
I'd rather take the lead

I cannot be captured
Influenced
Or changed
My pieces, uncollectible
Refuse to be arranged

You hope I'll be receptive
Willing and susceptible
But I would rather stand-alone
Than change to fall in step with you.

35

Scattered black
Across the staff
The bar lines, hard to read
I sit, upright and mighty
Against the ivory keys

Complicated chords
Elaborate dexterity
This music sheet, so intricate
A classical complexity

Yet, still composed so perfectly

A masterpiece so maddening
As outrageous as they say
Even to a worthy pianist...

I'm impossible to play.

36

"…I can wrangle the rising sun
As it illuminates the lands
Cast a line and reel it in
Then cradle it in my hands

My facets cast the cosmos
Shedding stardust while I stride
My body is a universe
I've got galaxies in my eyes

Like the moon, I control the tides…"

Darling, I am where magic resides.

37

Droplets race against the glass
Across from white, they fall
The steady beat of silent rain
My shadow on the wall

Peacefully, it hangs its head
As if to rest unseen
Maybe this means I'm finally still

Or

Is nothing as it seems?

38

I live inside my mind
I've got a world that's all set up
It makes the perfect sense to me
So, in my head...*I'm stuck*

I dance outside the doorway
Of real world and mentality
Sadly
What I tell myself

Will never match reality...

39

I will be a shooting star
The brilliant passing light
Beautiful, for a moment
Before flashing out of sight

Your hopeful eyes
Search the sapphire skies
Caught in the diamond web
Wishing on lingering stardust

That someday, I'll pass by again.

40

Conversations with strangers at coffee shops
Cappuccinos and not enough seats
Crowded stations, filled with faces
Busy sidewalks and bustling streets

Overlooked
Underappreciated
Small things, we used to ignore
The value in "everyday" moments
Unnoticed

That is, until they're gone.

41

*Randomly standing
in front a scene
of what seems to be
two horses.*

A strikingly white Arabian
Majestically still, in frame
Unbridled and unbothered
Standing opposite of a cage

A valiant Stallion
Black as coal
Eyes engulfed in rage
It stamps in fury
Behind the bars
Trapped inside the cage

The Stallion dreams to be released
The Arabian stands in place
Free by will yet stagnant
As the black horse plans escape

You observe these mighty beasts
Analyze the scene
Nothing odd about it
They're the same...

Or so it seems.

When you shift positions
Stop looking and start seeing
Your perception of the bars
Now seems inherently deceiving

Rearrange your stance
Step aside and look between them
Notice...
One is still a horse
But the other is a zebra

A befuddling discovery
When at last, you solve the riddle
This optical illusion
Gives you something to consider:

If you're the zebra, locked inside
Break free
And be *perceptive*
Because life is what you make of it

And it's all about perspective.

42

"What are your strengths and weaknesses?"

Well, to me
They are one and the same
Summed up well
In just 3 words:

Intellectual
Innocent
Insane

43

The finding of familiar eyes
That cannot be defined
An unexpected impact;
When unknown souls collide.

44

A musician crosses paths with a poet
It didn't seem worth it to know him
A sentence he sang
Stuck the wrong chord
But fit perfectly into a poem

"You'd probably fall deeply in love
And that's a bad thing you see
I don't want the next book you write
To end up all about me.."

The rhythm stung an open wound
She bowed her head and prayed
It wasn't the words that hurt the most

It was truth, so bluntly conveyed..

So, away she stayed
To heal in the shade
Let it silently fade
Write away all her pain

The beauty of time—
perspective can change.

And maybe....they both had it wrong.
See, we all cross paths for a reason
It doesn't always end in sorrow
Why pen him as the villain?
When she could write him as a hero?

45

Spilling through the window
As morning breaks the sky
The sunlight hits my weathered neck
And then, I catch your eye

You gaze upon my faded frets
Worn from years of strum
Melodies mixed with memories
Gentle fingers, come and gone

You take me down, and tune me
Think back on how we've grown
Time has slowed your fingers
Yet, you try for one last song

Reminisce our greatest hits
Your awkward learn-to-play
Years and years of practice
As brown turned wisps of gray

Melodically, remember me
Brand new
You brought me home
The songs you sang to sadness
Love and life, composed

Your sweeping thumb, across my strings
Plucks the tunes of time
Notes and chords of yesterday
A life-long lullaby
Moments played in perfect pitch
The years, have come and passed
Calloused fingers grip the pick
Now, master of the craft

Then, you place me on the wall
Your wrinkled smile, softened
A nod, for all the best of times
Acoustics

Unforgotten.

46

Divine horizon
Indigo tides
Ivory foam that clings to the sand
Salt speckled skin
Sun kissed cheeks
The gulls that govern the land

The crackle of rocks
As the waves roll back
The hum of a hovering plane
I'll continue to dream of the sun and sea

Until we meet again.

47

Trust the heart, trust the feeling

It's the beat that will speak through your chest

But the mind always tries to say otherwise

I wish to think more and feel less.

48

Draped in beams of silver
A moonlit silhouette
What lies inside those musing eyes?

How to forgive...
How to forget....

49

Rising sun, morning hush
Surrounded by cloudless abyss
These concrete trees are closing in
Sparkling glass and bricks

Receiving a sign in falling white
A lonely feather in the wind
It sings,

"You must be greeted by an ending..
Before anything new can begin."

Solemnly, accepted
Declared by the crow as it cries
A peaceful breeze kisses my cheeks

And away the feather flies.

50

God Said...

"The stars were an accident. The sun was so blinding…

I tripped over Earth and dropped a handful of diamonds."

51

It lingers in the air like a whisper
A soft secret, light as a feather
Floating up and around
It is always felt
But stays inherently unnoticed
Or simply, ignored
For to be acknowledged?
No, that would be chaos
Upsetting the delicate balance of what is
Challenging the carefully plotted points on the maps of our lives
Scrambling them, casting them from their order
Scattering them around us
No, it's best to let it settle above us
Its place in our world is that of a light fog
Resting peacefully above our heads
Never quite heavy enough to weigh us down
And maybe one day, that fog will clear
Dissolving seamlessly into the universe around us
Surrounding us
Finding its place to finally make sense
But if it never leaves the sky above
And stays just close enough to still feel its presence
Well, my friend
I pray you'll know it's there.
For lingering in the air like a whisper is...

I love you.

52

Back and forth
To and fro
Teetering with their choices
Indecisive by design
Ask questions, they freeze, voiceless

Swinging like a pendulum
From one side to the other
Traipsing between options
Choosing makes them shudder

Smothered by conflictions
Constant hesitation
Never sure how to proceed
A carousel of vacillation

Their ever changing mind state
Can't settle on decisions
These beings they love to temporize
No matter what conditions

Who are these dubious critters?
These maniacal, uncertain brutes?
The ones who dwell unknowingly
And dream of absolutes

Meet the oscillating beings
Faceless, restless, creatures
Undecided, hiding out
With alternating features

They live in every one of us
Deep in our subconscious
Compelling us to second guess
Approach our lives with caution

The oscillating beings
Beaten by free will
They'll fall away, defeated
If you decide to choose.

53

A constellation once told me a story
How love sent him over the moon
He said, "Tell me your wish.
My arrow won't miss…
Believe and it's sure to come true!"

I screamed at the skies for telling me lies
Cried out for my wishes misplaced
Frantically searched
Only to find

The constellations had all been erased.

54

Hope Against Heart

The sidewalk
Spilled coffee
Painful pause
Silence
The key clicks the lock

Hopeful breath
One last glance
Heart screams

"Don't look back."

55

The iron boar in a city of steel..
A man-made miracle
Grotesque and immense

A beast out of place, cast from order
A presence that doesn't make sense

The wild boar in a concrete jungle
Demanding attention from all
Keeping a watchful eye
over each passerby
Its purpose:
To exist and enthrall

A centerpiece
Masterpiece
Head turning fellow
A stop-dead-in-your-tracks
Intriguing beast

Drawing you in to be captured
His favorite game of catch and release

An odious beast forged from beauty
Such a wondrous feast for the eyes
He stands motionless
Collecting your countenance

Curious stares, as you ask yourselves,

"Why?"

"Why here? In this place?"
"What's his purpose?"
The lingering bystanders' plea

Yet, the iron boar—
Tight-lipped and majestic

Knows his allure lies within mystery.

56

I have never been wanted
Never been loved
Chased, adored, or caressed
I've only been grabbed from the end of the bar
Taken home, left alone, and undressed

Never been held past morning
Been kissed on the lips by love
For me, it seems to always end
Just as quickly as it had begun

I only know moments
A fluttering heart
The joy of a passing glance
A bittersweet taste of romance
In a seconds-long, elegant dance

I am no stranger to, "See you soon"
To me, it means, "Never again"
And I have been told, over and over
"You make such a wonderful friend."

Nothing more and nothing less
I walk this path alone
Stumbling along, lost in my mind
Hoping to find the "the one."

I never have.

57

There are two things that save a soul
One is hope and the other is love
These are things you must find in yourself
Grasp them, and never give up

The good and bad, it comes in waves
And although it's quite easy to drown
You will find okay
If you ride it out
And refuse to let life knock you down

It's the light at the end of a tunnel
And the promise of a new tomorrow
Even the tiniest sliver of hope
Is enough to lift spirits from sorrow

Hope is a funny fellow
Overshadowing fear and hate
When you trust the voice within
They can not dominate

And that dear friends is the message
Keep hanging on, don't give up
Becuase even with the smallest glimmer of hope
There's nothing you can't overcome.

58

The cellists straighten into position
Violinists grasp their bows
Elegant gowns and fresh pressed linen
Gracefully stand in rows

And so, the music flows
The maestro nods and sways
Twirling bodies fill the room
And I, remain in place

Between the dancing lace and faces
You somehow catch my gaze
Approaching in slow motion
As I watch the gliding maze

Surprising is your presence
You smirk
I blush
We smile
"May I have this dance," you say
"I've watched you for a while"

Your palm, outstretched
The symphony plays
I take your hand in mine
We fall in step
To ivory tune
A waltz through passing time

Forever in one moment
The ballroom slowly wanes
Around us falling minutes
Seconds
Hours
Days

Decades

The music plays and the maestro sways
One two, one two, step stop
A melodic embrace, we move with haste
Knowing soon, we'll have to part

Two steps back
Then, four steps back
An unbreakable passionate gaze
The bittersweet end to our first and last waltz

As the symphony silently fades.

The people begin to mingle
For a moment we stand in place
You take a silent snapshot of my soul
And say,

"I'll always remember your face."

Diana

Forever
You are in the sun
As it rises over the seas
In every beautiful feather
Floating in the breeze

In every bird that glides the sky
Beneath its weightless wings
In the glory of the sunset
And in the peace in which it brings

All of the songs that nature sings.

In a flock of crimson cardinals
Your sweetness in their tunes
And in a marvelous emerald garden

You're in every rose that blooms

Forest creatures and fumbling bunnies
The deer that graze the grass
In the butterflies that kiss the wind
Gently, as they pass

In every graceful snowflake
Dancing slowly to the ground
In The flurries of white softly fall
That's where you'll be found

In every twinkling Christmas light
On the gold embellished wreathes
In the dazzling ornaments
That catch our eyes
As they sparkle on the trees

And in the autumn leaves
In the salty summer air
In every lyric leaving our lips
In every loving prayer

You're there

This beautiful world around us
You're in every wondrous part
Yes, like the sun, you shine everywhere

And stay forever in our hearts.

In memory of Diana Jean Nascenzi-Morocco

59

Two people on hill letting time pass by

He asked me,
"If you could go back in time, what would you change and why?

Staring out at the sky, I replied,
"I would say what's on my mind and I would rip off my disguise"

So, further he inquired:
"What changed and why?"

To my surprise, I realized:
I had grown wise between then and now.

I sighed,
"Besides the guise,
If you had asked me how I felt at that time
I would've bottled it up inside,
Incessantly denied,
And then…I would've lied. But, now…

"But now…?"

" I've broken every wall and I have nowhere left to hide.

…in other words, I'm not afraid because at least I'll know I tried"

60

I'm often inspired by the crystal abyss
A brilliant moon in an ocean of stars
Sometimes I ponder electrons
Or, how protons stay positively charged

Sometimes it hits
While I randomly sit
Looking into a galaxy of steel
Peering at checkerboard lights from a tower
Thinking…

"How in the world do I feel?"

It could be bird
Or a sandwich
A pile of trash on the street
Most of the time I'm inspired
By a stranger I randomly meet

But lately, I'm crazy and all bottled up
The engine inside has misfired
Quite possibly so, I may need a nap

I'm much too tired to be re-inspired.

61

Give me something to believe in
The world screams back
"Yourself"
I plead, "What am I not seeing?"
It said, "Stop measuring your wealth"

But, I'm tired, stuck, bound up, and blinded
Entangled like a rope
Show me something to believe in
Give me faith

I'm losing hope

Show me where the tunnel leads
I've been tripping through the dark
I'm not asking you to light the way
I need just the slightest spark

And the only thing that keeps me here are the words:

"Please don't give up"

It seems my faith was shaken
I'm bad at following my heart
My mind got us lost on the journey

Before it could even start

I know that seeing isn't believing
It's a *feeling*
And I'm learning to trust

So even when I am shown nothing at all

I'm never going to stop.

There's a sentence of hope
That slices the ropes
And makes the end of tunnel visible

"You feel like giving up the most,
Right before you get your miracle. "

62

I can't expLain exactly what it is
I don't knOw what it means
Or, if it eVen truly exists
Yet, I beliEve in it.

63

Where is my happiness?
I softly whispered to the moon
It was a prayer that danced among the stars
And found its way to you

I love to hear your heart beat
My cheek pressed to your chest
Lose track of time beside you
Freeze the seconds as they pass
Maybe save a minute…

Just to catch my breath

I find it in your laughter
In your voice and in your mind
In every passing moment
Where our souls have intertwined

As if the stars aligned
For your path to cross with mine

Dare I say, for once I feel
This restlessness is eased
At peace as if I'm with myself
As impossible as that seems

See, happiness is me
And you
So, let me feel it all and more
Because dare I say, after lifetimes...

It was you I was praying for.

64

Yes, it's all true...*I will write about you*

Taste the words as they dance between breaths
Savor each sentence, kiss every letter
As they fall, let the ink stain my lips

I desire to describe you as fire
I'm inspired
By your passion that flickers within
Warrior spirit, wild lion
Magnetic and drawing me in

I'd write how you mirror the moonlight
Illuminating and intense
How even through darkness
You still seek the light
In silver script
I'd admire your strength

I wish to write while wrapped up in your presence
I'm not sure why this all feels so wrong
I know that it's best to move on
Leave it alone

So, I'll pen you as the love that almost was
At least inside my mind...
I'll set you free, stare out at the sea
But always wish that your heart could be mine

Yes, I'll write and then rip up the pages
I understand that when push comes to shove
Even a beautiful poem

Wouldn't make you and I fall in love...

See, that would be a miracle

Entirely, against all odds.

65

No, I don't want to say it
No, I can't face the words
So, yes, I'm going to bottle it up
And act as if nothings occurred

But then, the pressure gets worse
And my soul is screaming in tongues
I take a deep breath and I hold it
Grip the wheel and let pain burn my lungs

No, I don't want to feel it
It's something I don't understand
I reach for the phone and I hold it
But it fumbles, and falls from my hand

This was all so unplanned
And I'd rather pretend...
No I don't want to say it
The bottle expands

No, I don't want feel it
These are cards I'm unwilling to deal
I can't face it
I'm scared to admit it
And then...
If I say it

It's real

I'm gripping this wheel
I'm terrified to feel
It took me a lifetime
To finally heal...
I can't risk a heartbreak
I'd rather conceal
Bottle it up
Twist it shut
Leave it sealed

But it's bubbling up to the surface
An explosion that jumps through my bones
Electrically pulsing from heart to the veins
And I find myself losing control

Oh no

So, I guess…. that I'm going to feel it
Maybe it's best to just feel
I shake up the bottle
Open the cap

Guess it's time to let God take the wheel.

66

Caught in the thought
"It's too good to be true."
Overwrought
Over questioning blessings

I can't seem to trust
What's good and what's not
I'm too accustomed to life and it's lessons

To me, "Dreams come true"
Sounds a-lot like *deception*

I'm stressed by confessions
In need of expressing
I fall to my knees
As I'm begging the heavens

What is the truth?
I've run out of suggestions
Is it my mind playing tricks?
Is it just sickly obsessions?

I watch my thoughts scatter
In different directions....

They rise and fall as joy and fear
In essence, my soul believes in it all
But my mind shouts

"You'd better be beware!"

"Life is not fair"

"Nobody cares"

Oh dear

Stabbing my myself with sabotage

Though my reality is something *I choose*
I have to believe that it's all meant to be
If it's mine then there's nothing to lose

See risking it all could be my downfall
But I take chances against my perceptions
Because the only thing worse then losing it all

Would be turning my back on my blessings.

✸

67

What causes this confusion?
Is there a solution?
In this world of souls so disillusioned
Encased in concrete delusion…

Is it absolution or oblivion?

Guilty, as I too, once bound to the same insensibility
But those same chains shackled to my ankles
That kept me prisoner to the sea of stone
Are rusted, corroded, and all but gone

I heard a call

My solemn soul rises above the buildings
Blending with the blackened clouds of a brewing storm
Mighty and valorous
This vrmor constricts my chest
Breathless, I confess

"I do not understand how to conquer this great quest!
The battle of evil and material possessed!"

The golden hand of god appears
Stripping me of my fears
Drying my tears

He declares:

"I present you with a feathered pen. To mark the beginning, not the end.
Make them understand, we must make amends"

Peering down at wrath of the world below
I cry, "But, *why!*"

Confusion floods my eyes
The sun breaks the blackened skies

He replies:

"The pen is mightier than their swords.
This is a war to be won with words."

Within me he stirs

Rushing over the world as it slowly burns
Above the writhing violence it churns

The rivers of ink slowly flow

Revealing truth to the world below.

68

Love is a facade
Until it's not

Love is a fraud
Until it's not

Love is a farce
Until it's not

Love is unwelcome…

Until it knocks.

69

I am here and now
In my power
Strong
Wise
Driven

In my iris is fire and passion

To inspire the masses—*my vision*

I have conquered
Prevailed
I'm triumphant

I have risen from pain, I've endured
Standing tall
With my hardships behind me

On a road only paved by reward

I speak truth
I am valiant
And present
To make change
I am ever determined
Though I've carried the world on my shoulders

I stand proudly before you with purpose.

- 88 -

--- ✷ ---

I had a vision of the ending...

Isle of Skye

It glistened just like the ocean
Sparkled itself into view
I was standing alone looking out at the heavens
Diamond facets and dazzling blue

Suddenly beside me, a shadow took its place
Someone was there to join me
An unrecognizable face

Yet, we embraced...

It was you and I on the Isle of Sky
Wrapped in the golden haze
The backdrop, that brilliant horizon
We stood, shrouded by the sun and its rays
Locked in a gaze

At last, at peace with existence
Past the world and its wicked ways
At the top, this is it, and it's glorious

We've made it to better days...

Finally.

...the end is...

...the beginning...

Dear Reader,

There will come a time when you wake up one day and all of your worries and fears have suddenly fallen away. You begin to notice life's peaceful little details, like flower shops that line the sidewalk, birds resting on the fire escapes, and children skipping cracks on the concrete.

You'll notice how the sunlight can hit a building just right to make a brick shine. You'll hear the soft buzzing of insects wizzing by, once an irritating background noise…suddenly appreciated as a soothing hum.

You'll notice peoples faces—some cracked and worn from a lifetime of struggle, some fresh and youthful, some inviting and friendly, some angry and tired. But, you'll decide to smile at every one of them as they pass.

You'll notice how the rumbling of car engines, the chirping of birds, and the endless chatter of strangers conversations—all different sounds—somehow seem to create a beautiful symphony.

You suddenly realize that every little part of life is beautifully fascinating.

You suddenly realize that no matter what happens, it's all going to be okay.

You suddenly realize that even in an ugly world, there is something beautiful everywhere you look.

You suddenly realize that simply being alive is the greatest treasure.

You suddenly realize….

You have found happiness in everything.

You have found peace.

You are home.

Your story begins here. This is *your* moment. Take a leap of faith. Do whatever you want to do and keep going no matter who tries to get in your way. Don't wait for the right time.

The time is **now**.

Write your story. Write your goals. Write your thoughts.

Write the reality you wish to live...and then, *make it happen...*

The Contributors

Photo credit: *HXS (@HiddenBySoul) Colorblind, (July 30, 2021)*

About the Author

Natalie Nascenzi is a copywriter, poet, and author from Rhode Island. She moved to the city in 2017 to pursue her career in advertising. After a dramatic weight loss transformation of over 85 pounds and a journey through anxiety, depression, and loss of self, Natalie found herself again through words. Since then, she made an impression on New York City's open mic community and her works have been featured across the world in anthologies and independent publications.

From her first book *Out of Chaos* to now, Natalie has spread her message of hope and transformation and has continued the journey with readers through *The Aftermath of Unrest.* After her final installment of her poetry book series, *Isle of Skye,* Natalie plans to expand into the world of writing and beyond; carrying with her the mission to spread hope and postive change.

You can find her on Instagram: @nncenzi.

About the Artist

Nicolle DiIorio is originally from Long Island, New York but moved to Manhattan in 2013. Since then, she's worked as an Art Director and more recently began tapping back into her roots as an artist. This year, she started exploring different art styles and mediums. This led to the creation of her Instagram @draw_by_dip.

Nicolle's greatest joy artistically is capturing moments through her drawings. Now, she's found a way to merge her passion for the arts and making people smile by creating one-of-a-kind pieces in all mediums.

Other Titles by Natalie Nascenzi

"Out of Chaos"

ISBN: 978-0578644516

"The Aftermath of Unrest"

ISBN: 978-0578777665

"Write Yourself a Beautiful Day"

ISBN: 978-8501185135

For more information, visit www.natalienascenzi.com